IRISH FAIRY TALES

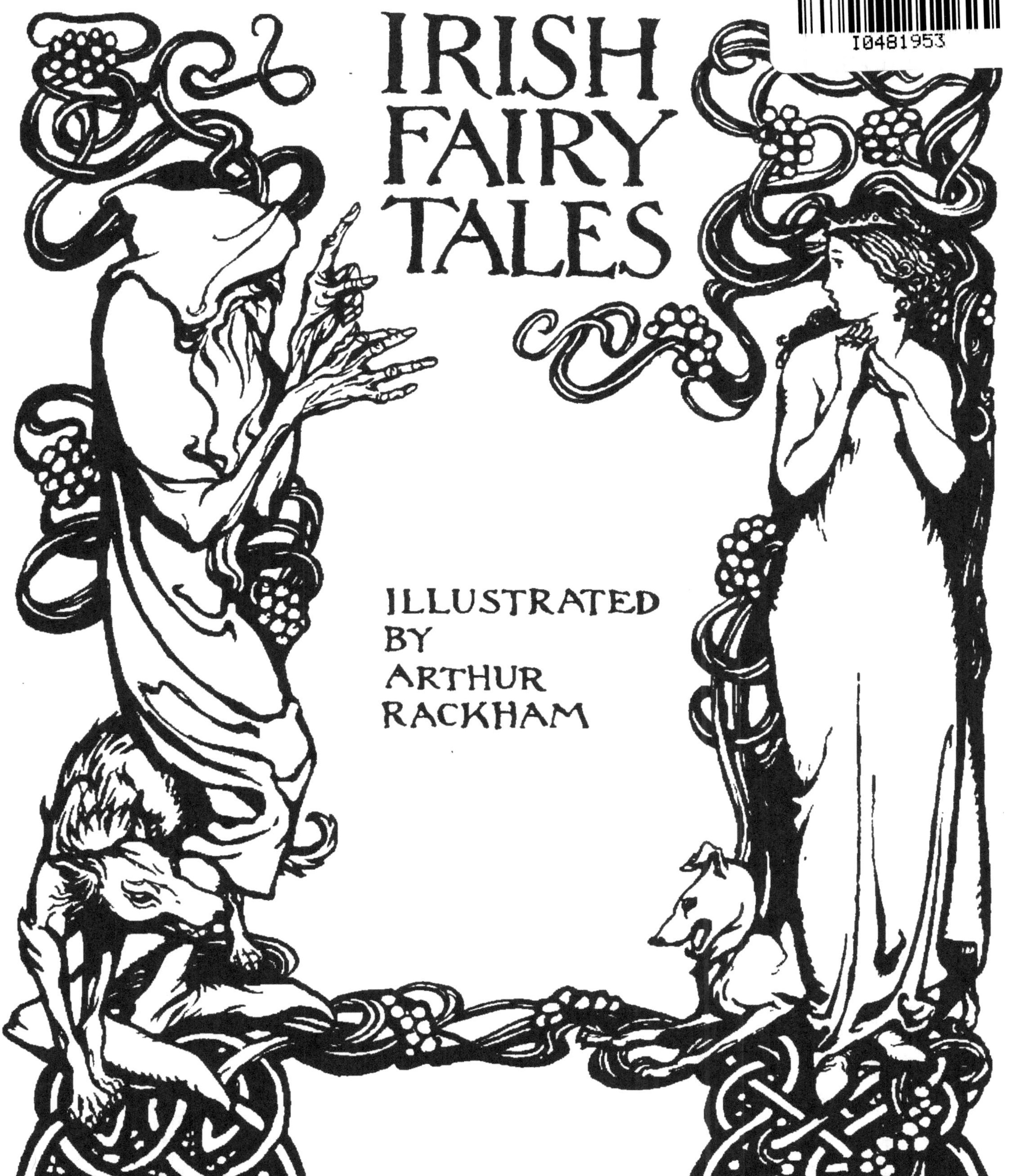

ILLUSTRATED BY ARTHUR RACKHAM

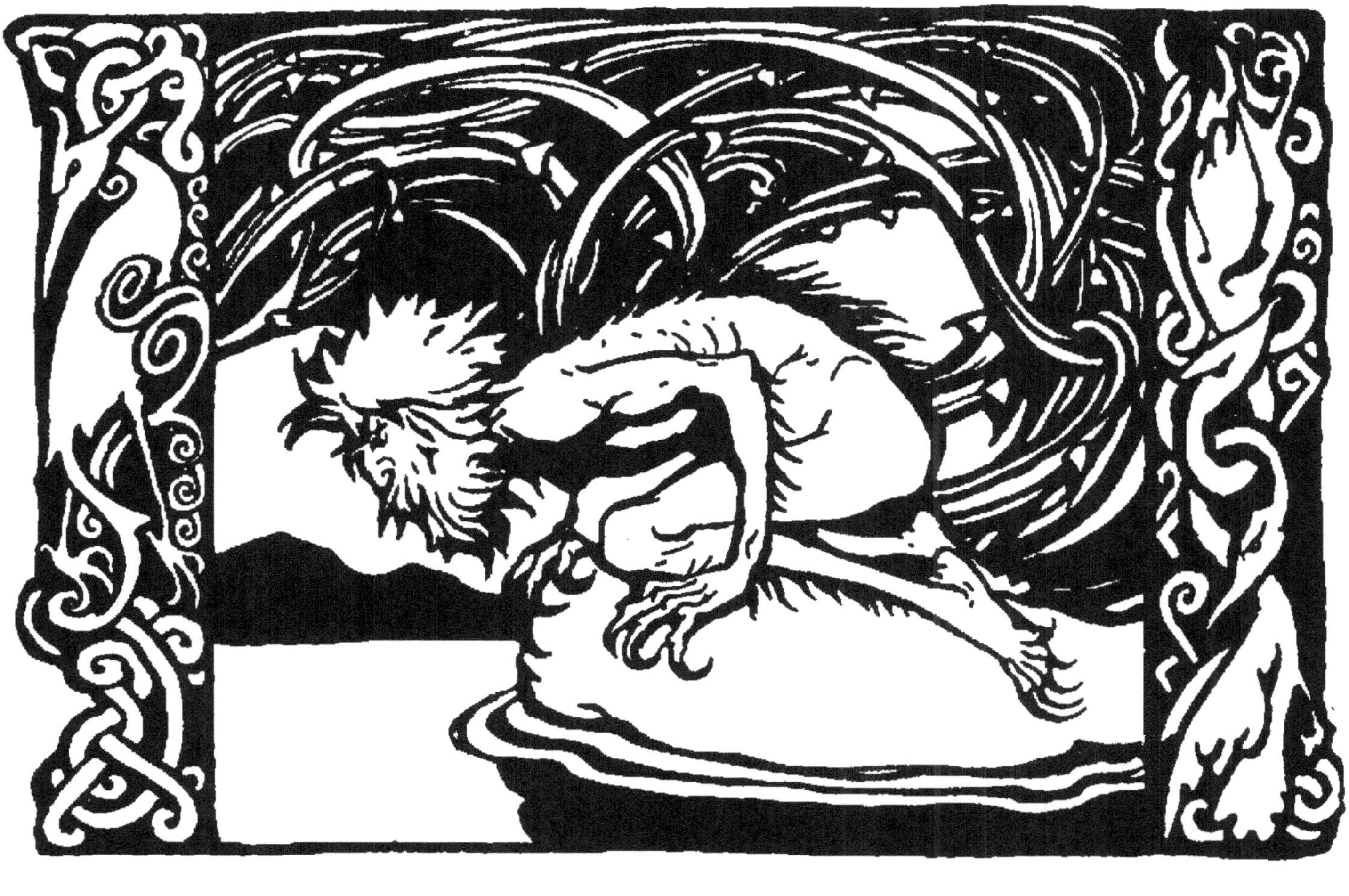

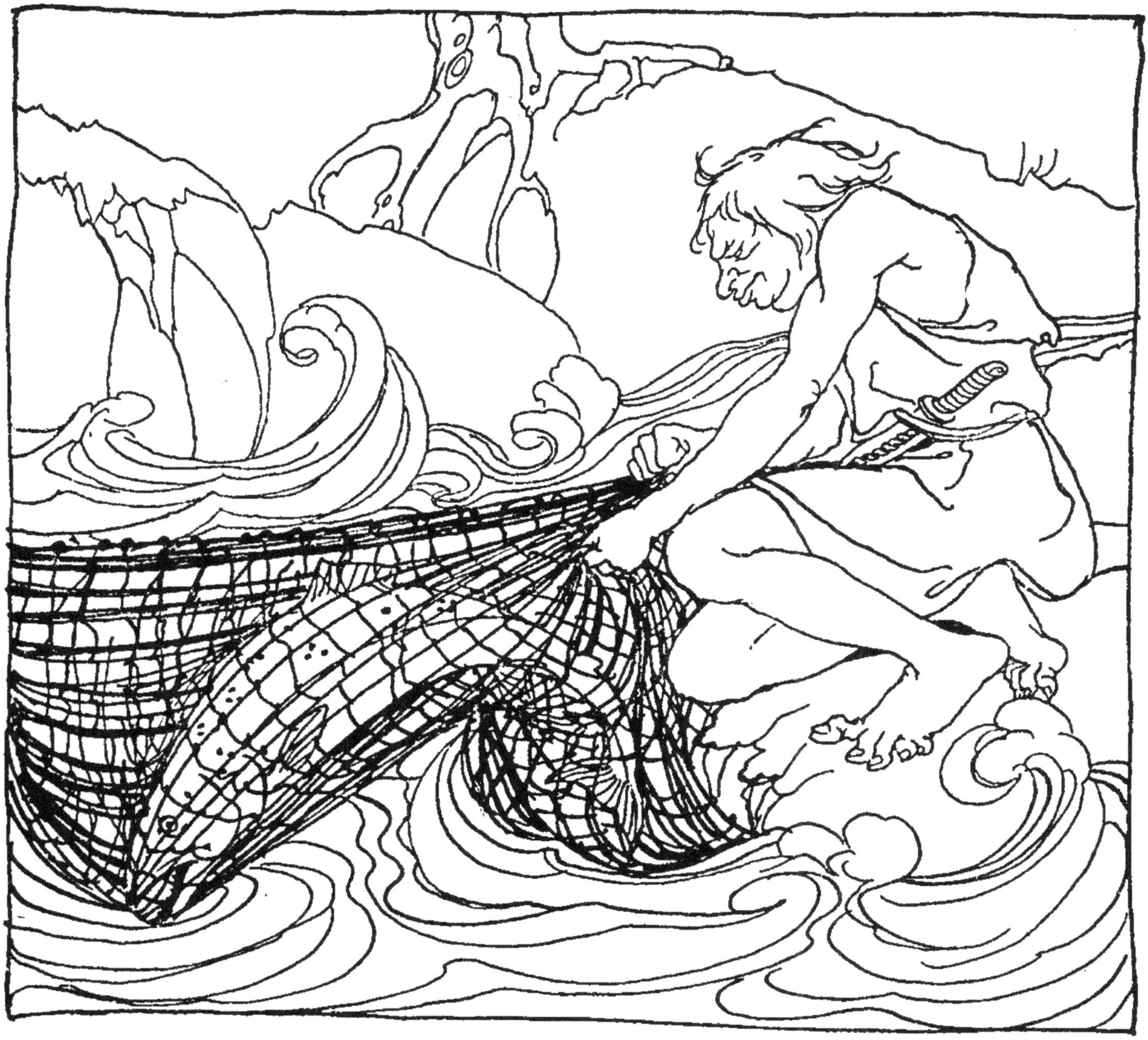

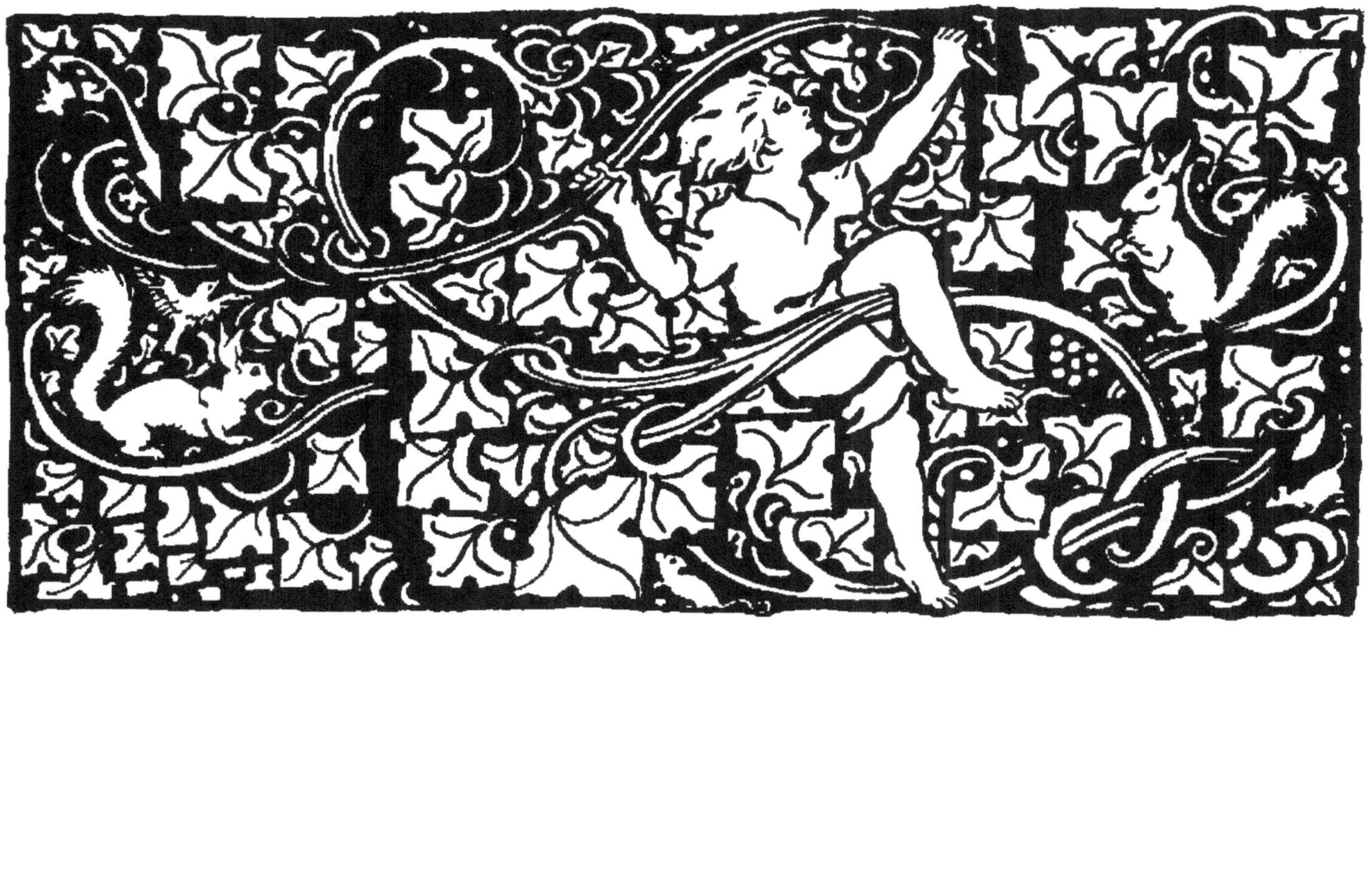

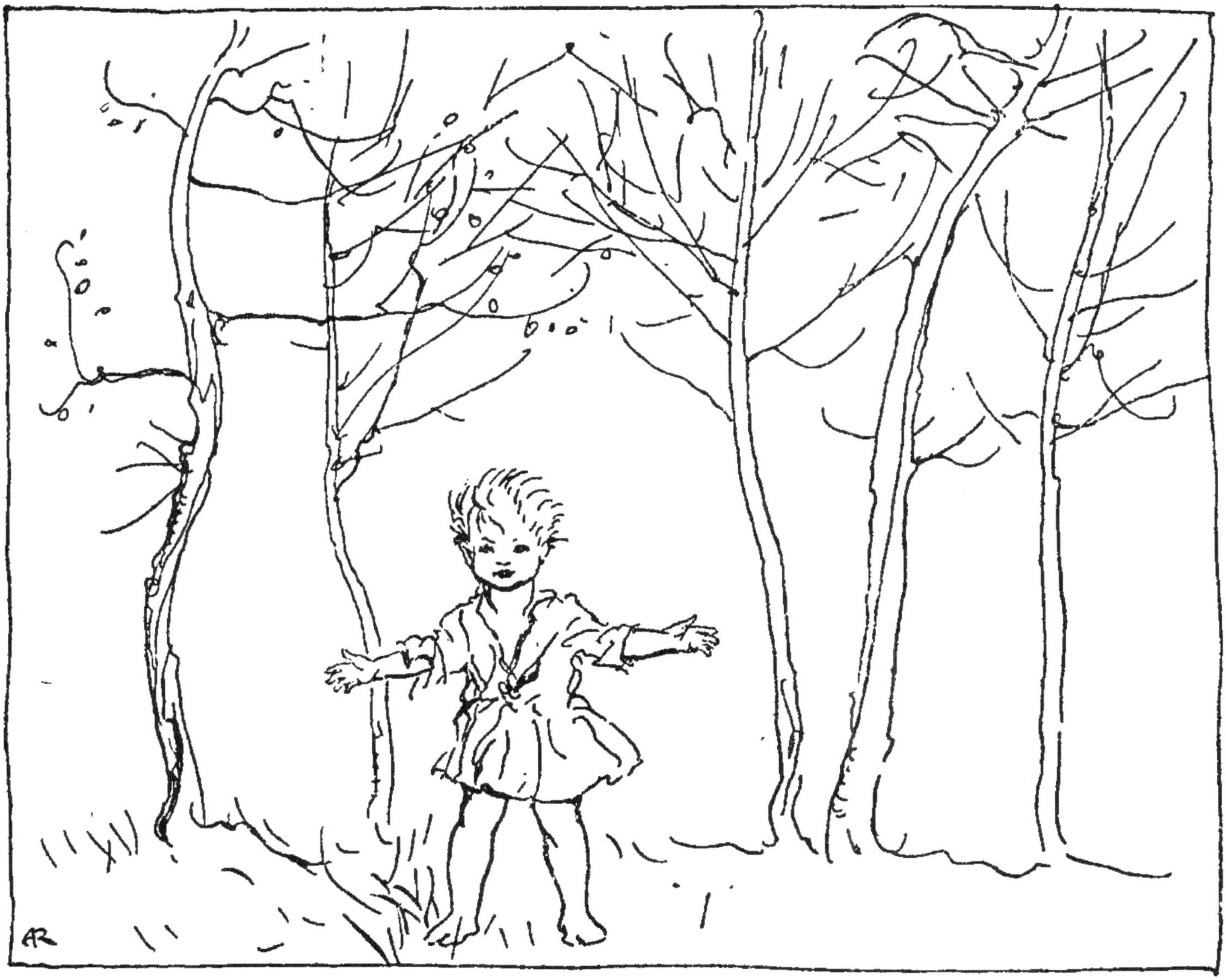

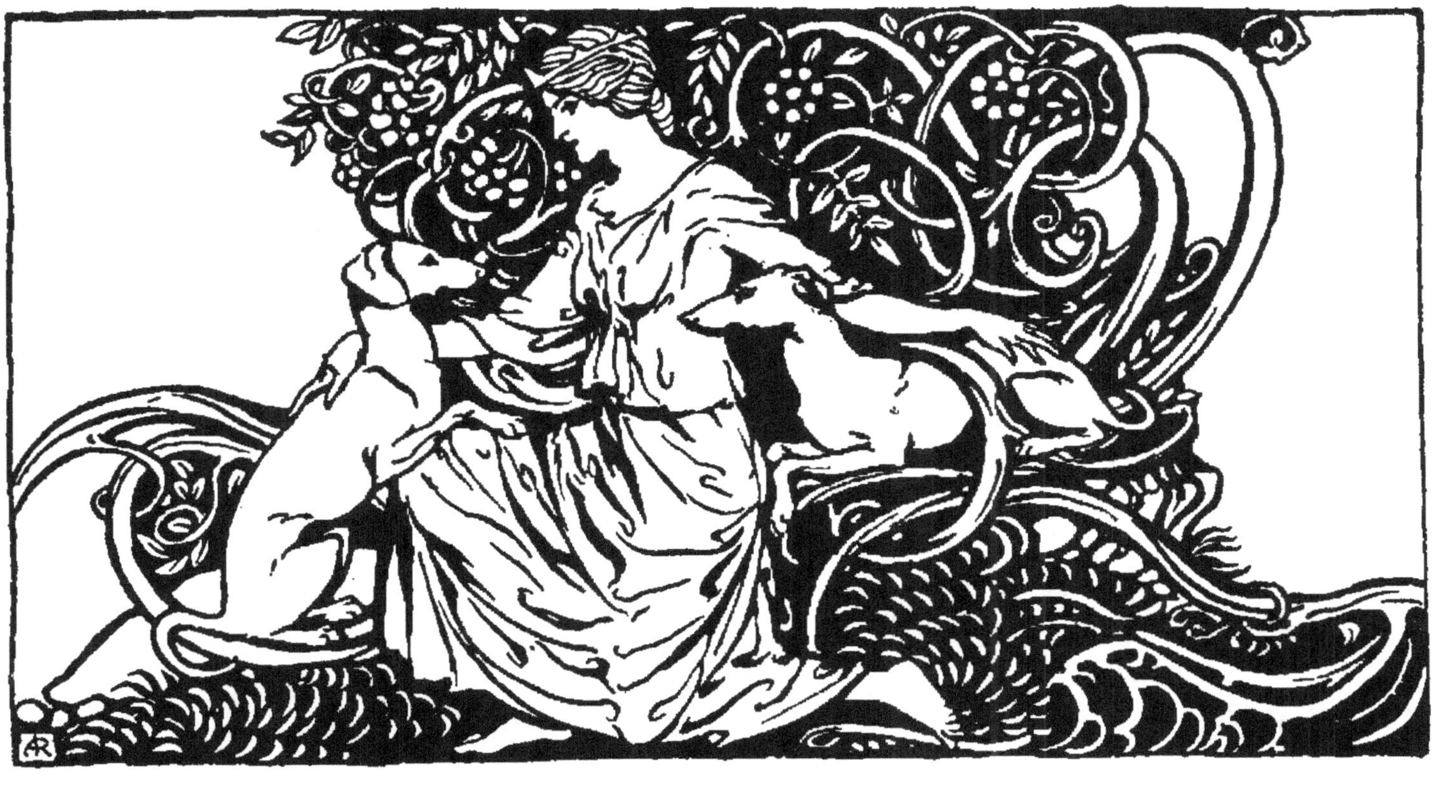
AR

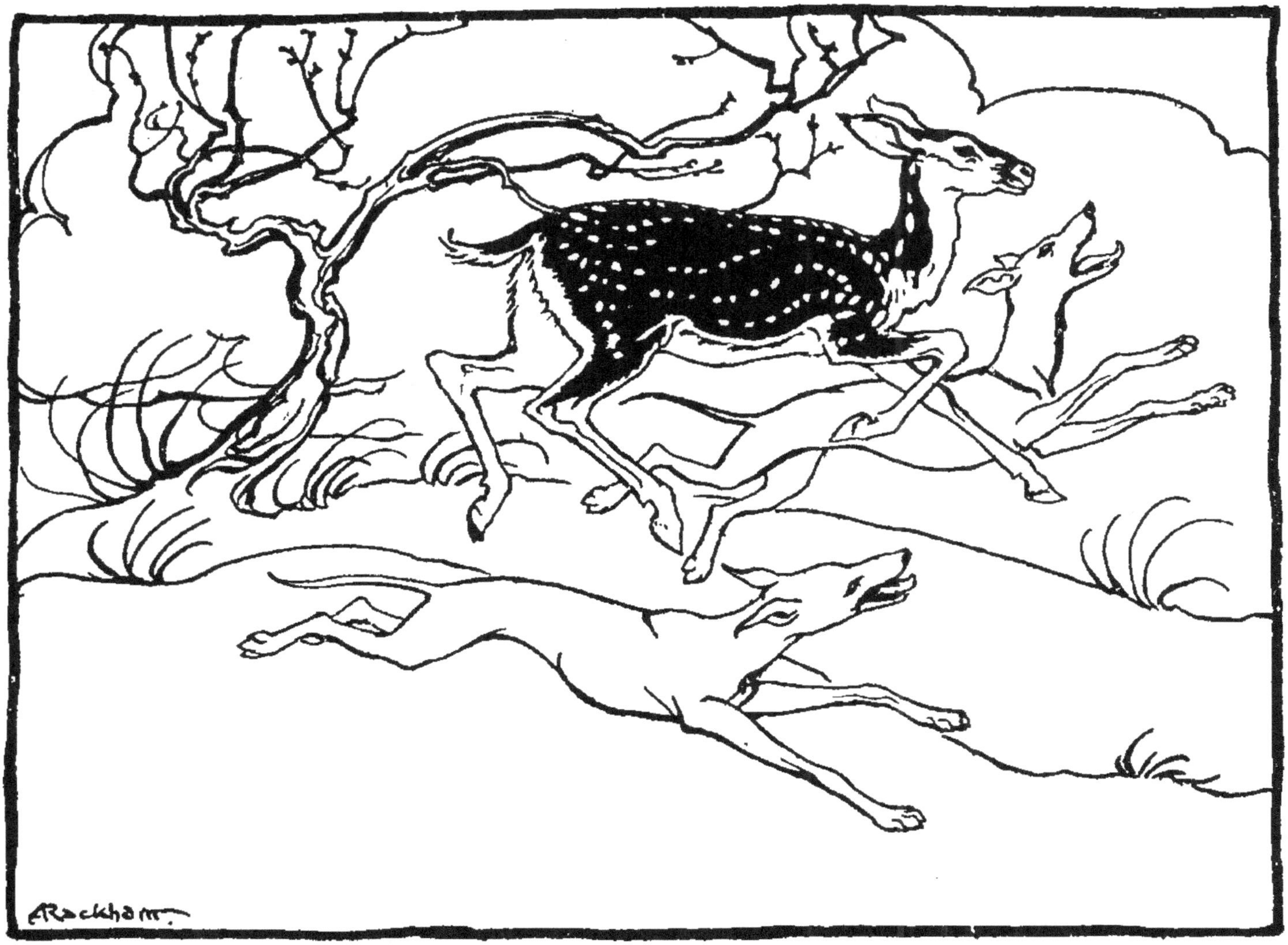
A Rackham

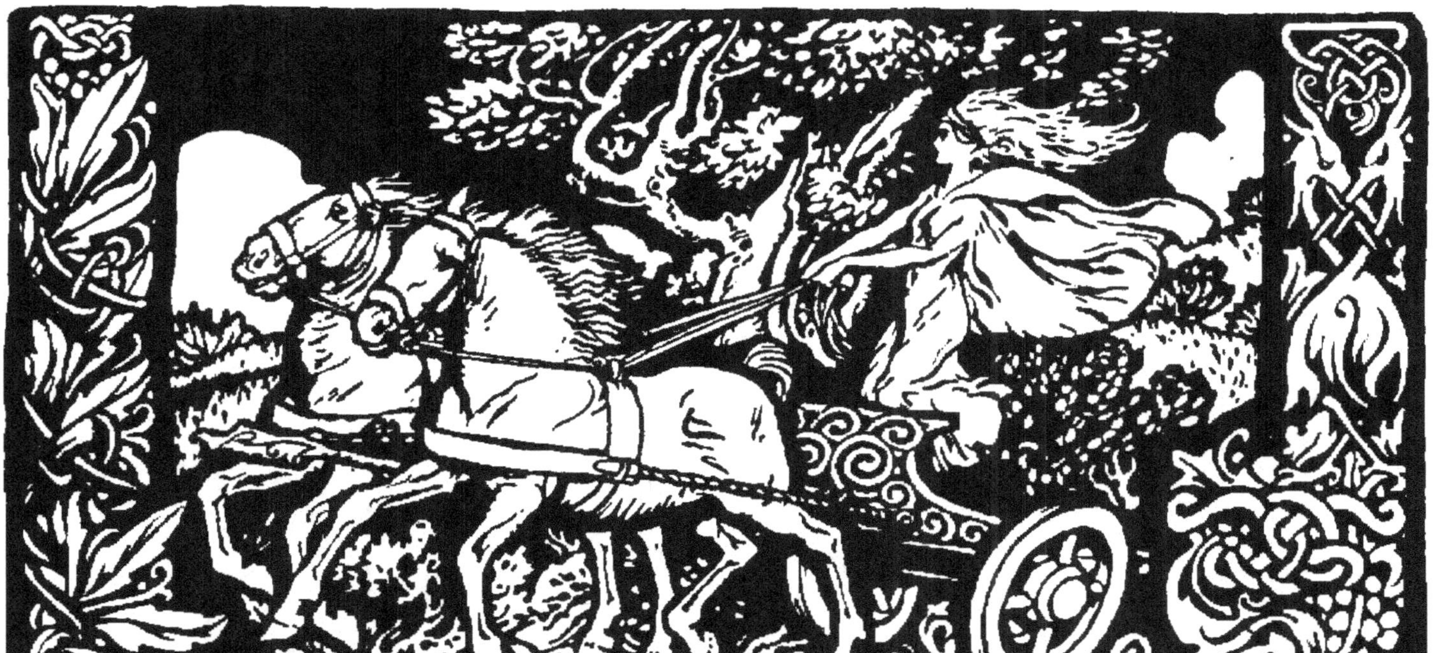

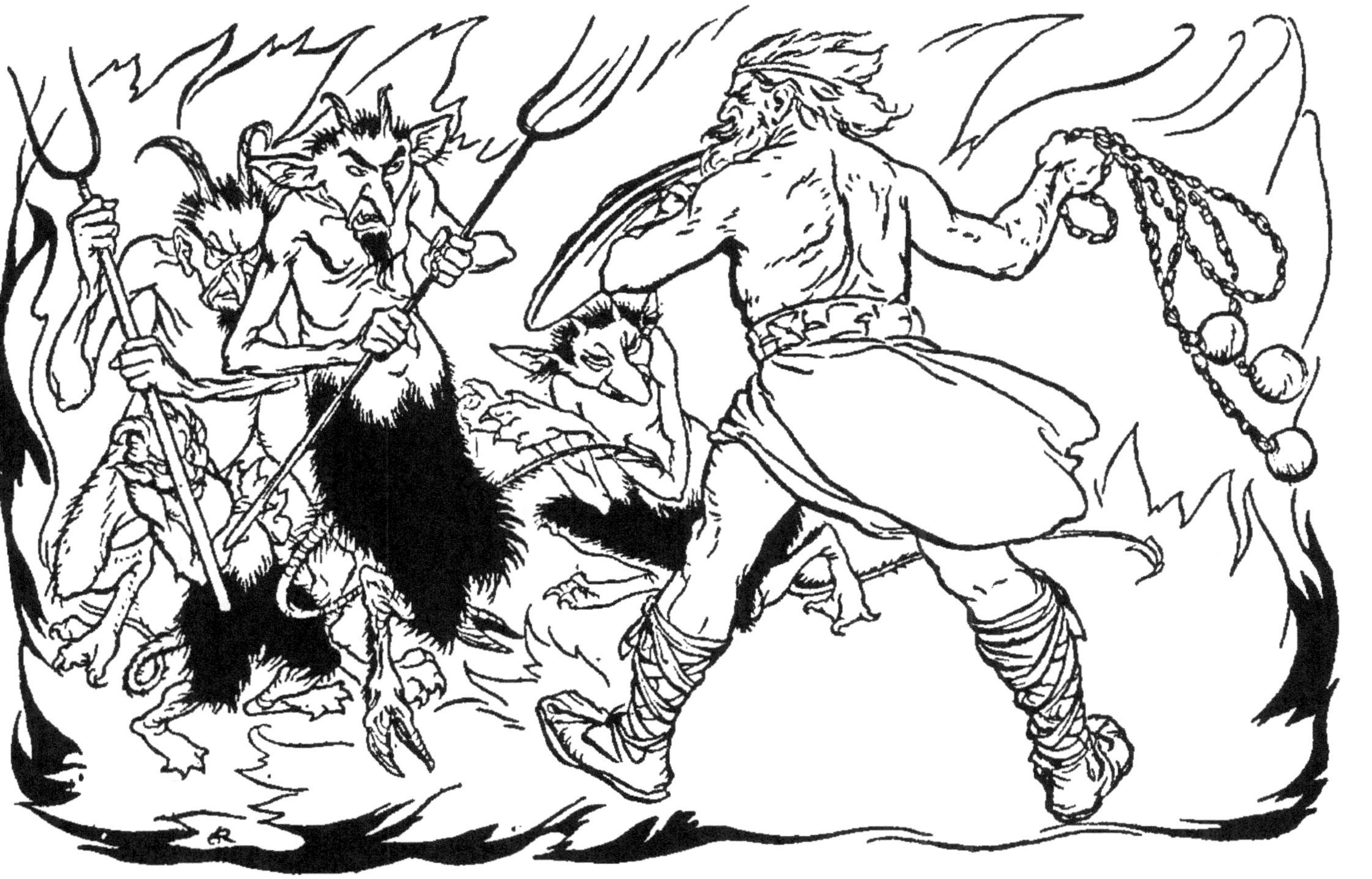

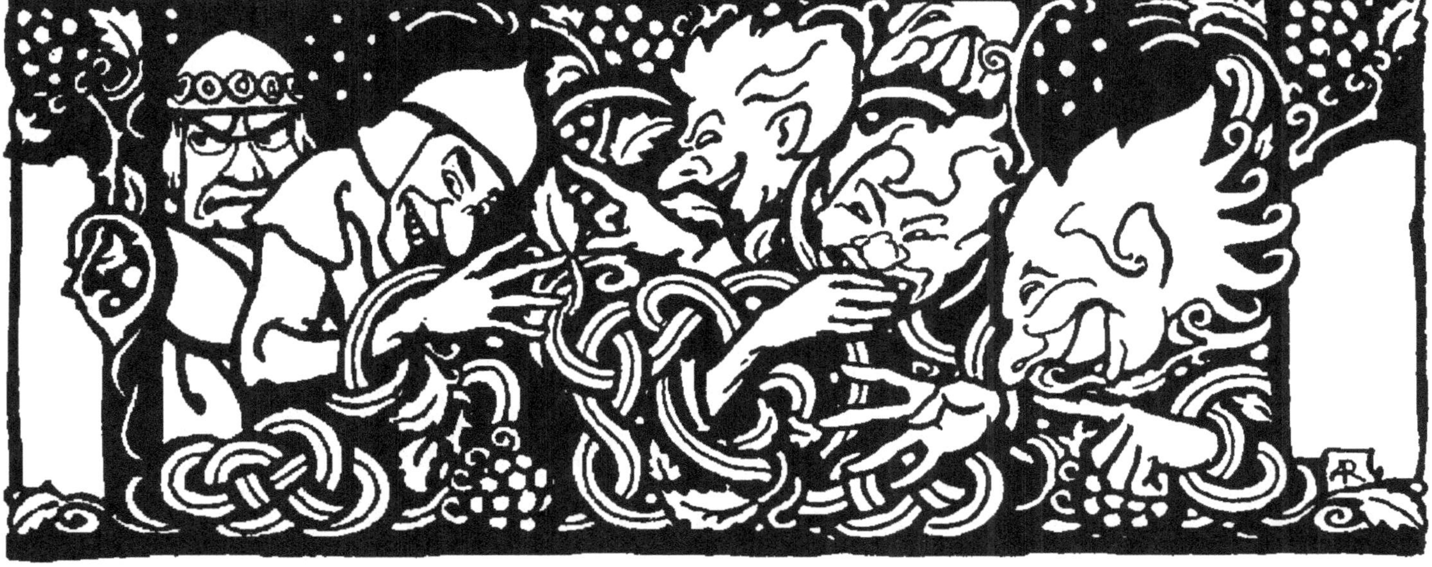

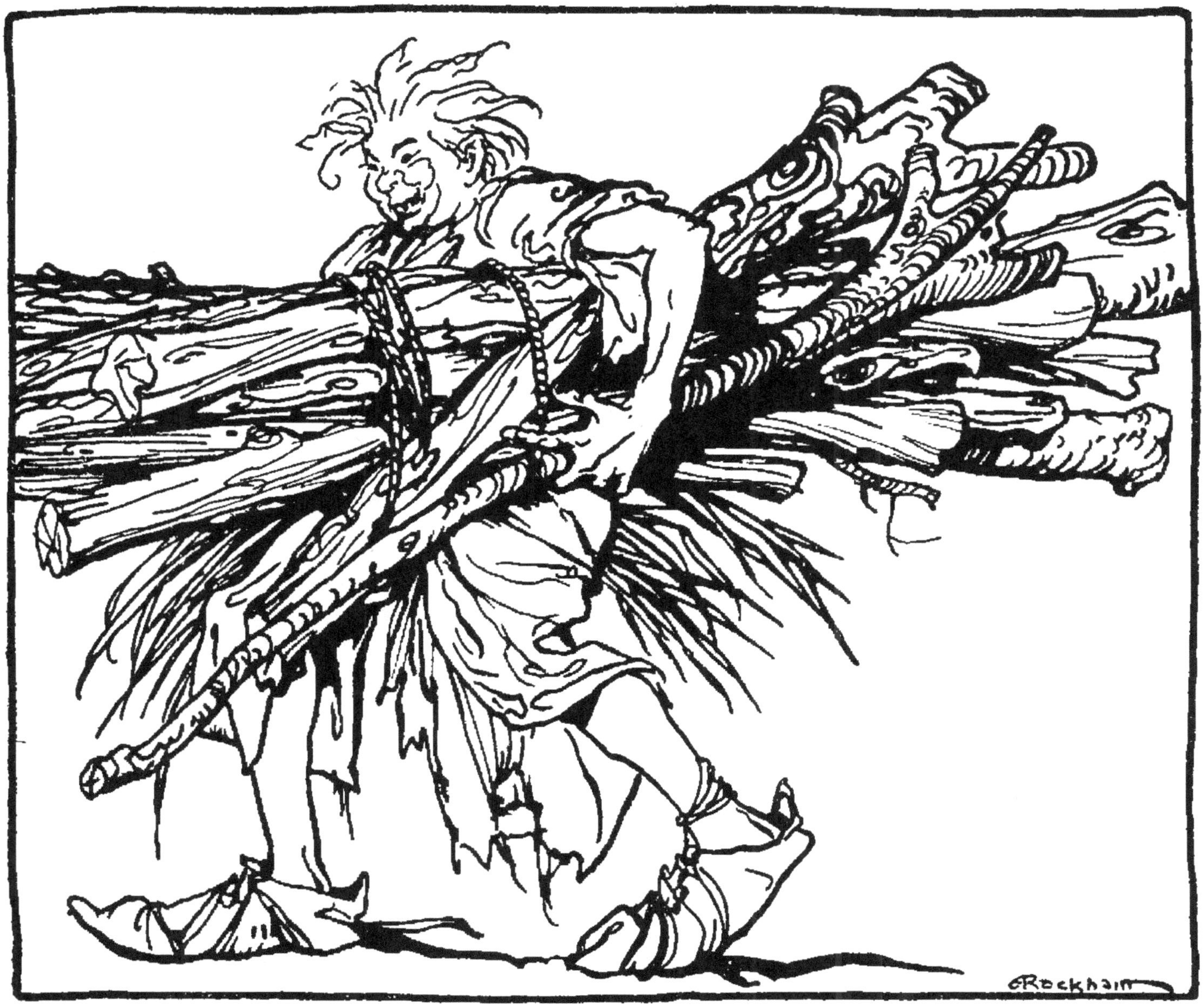

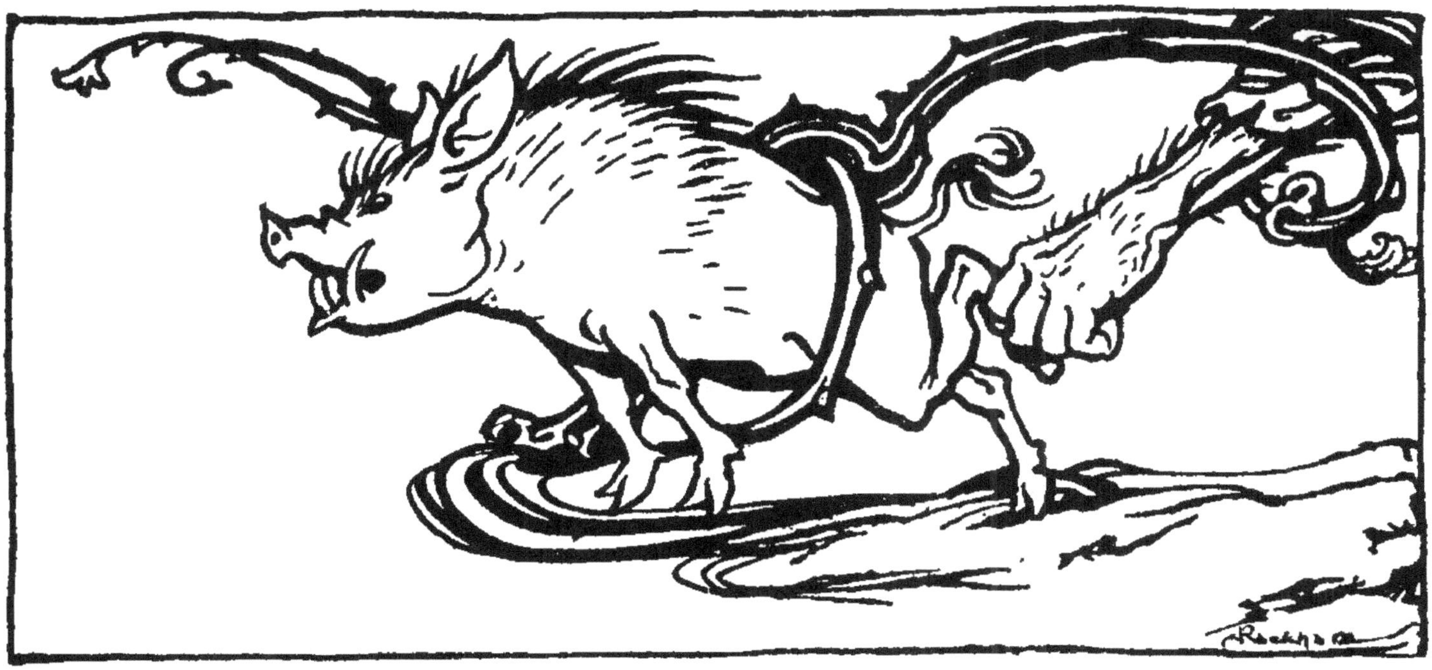

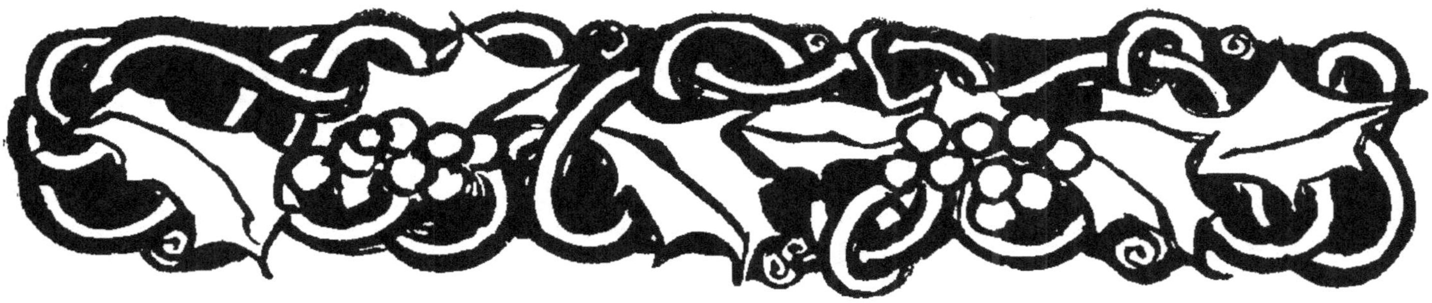

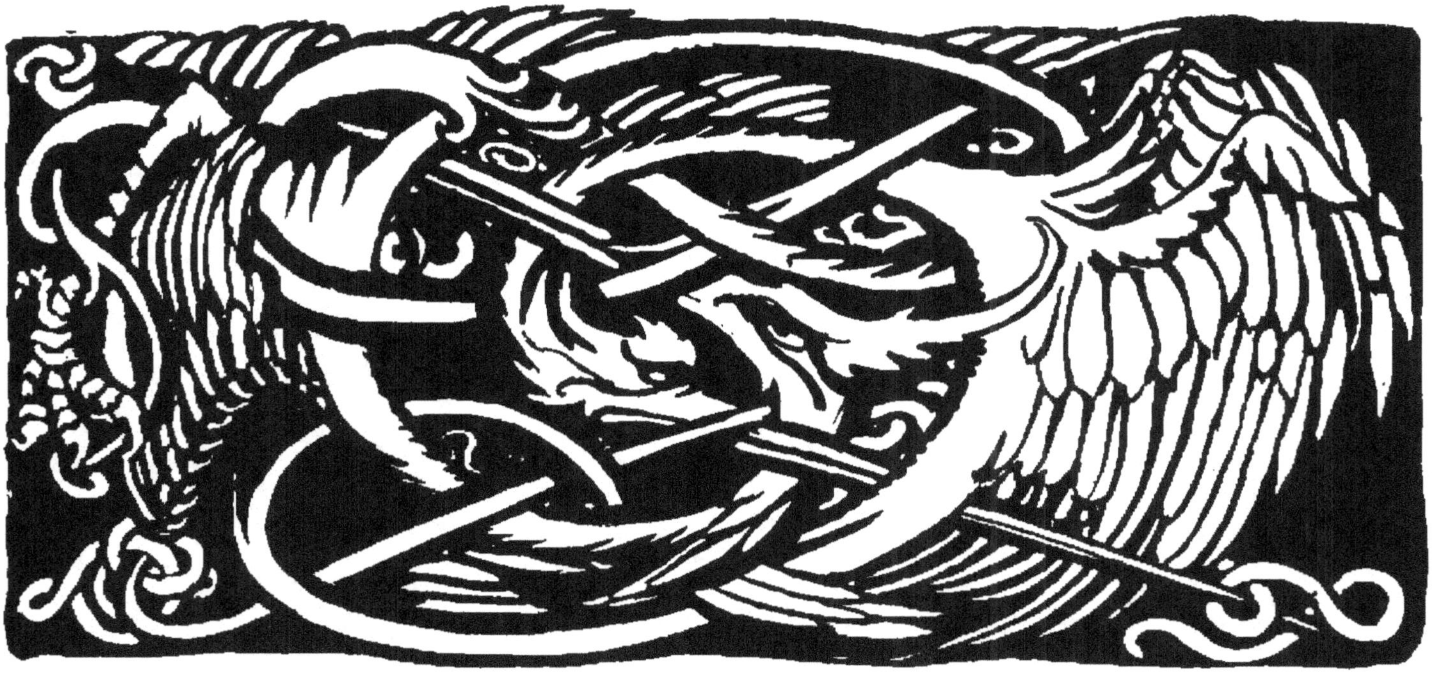

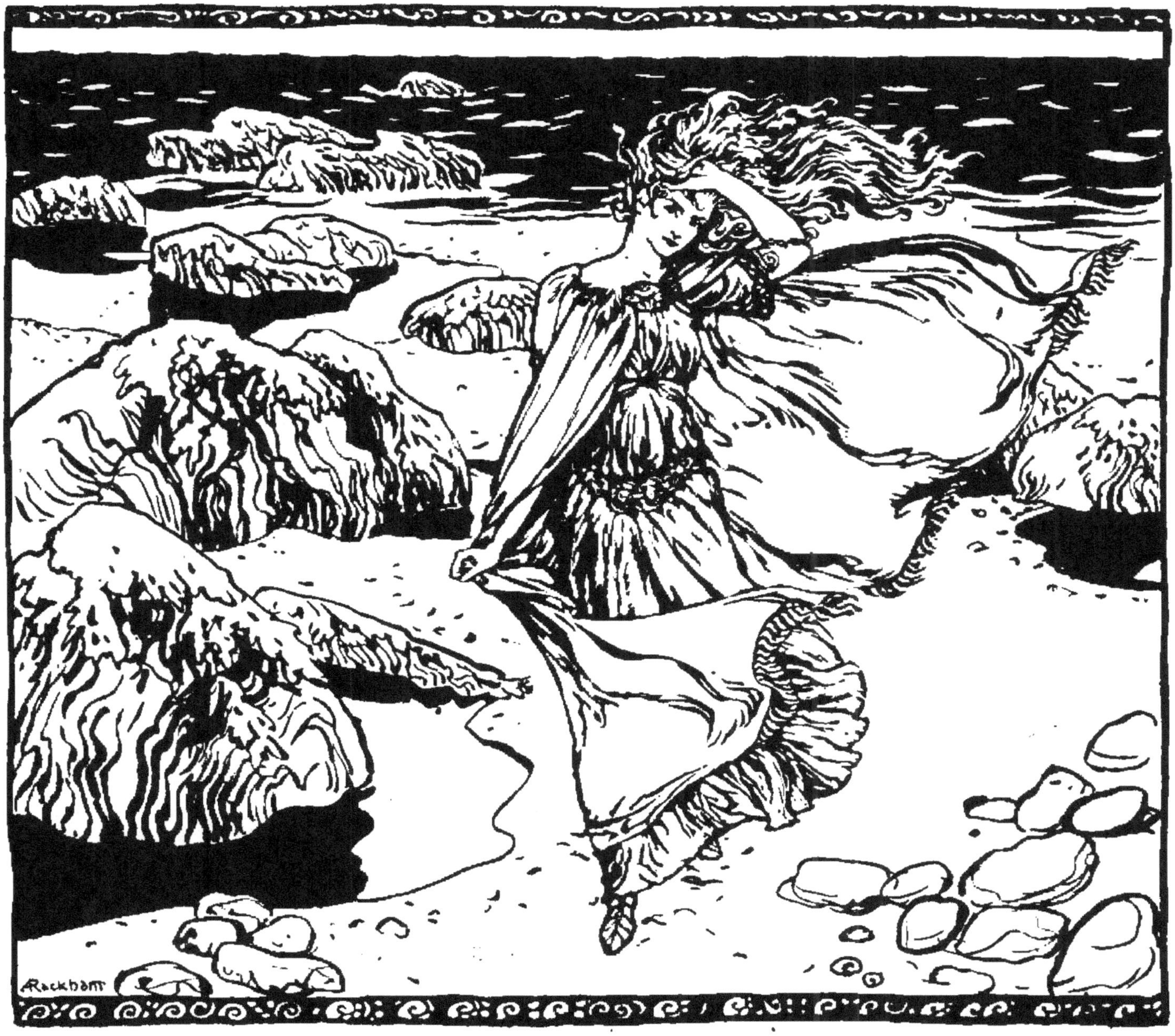
ARackham

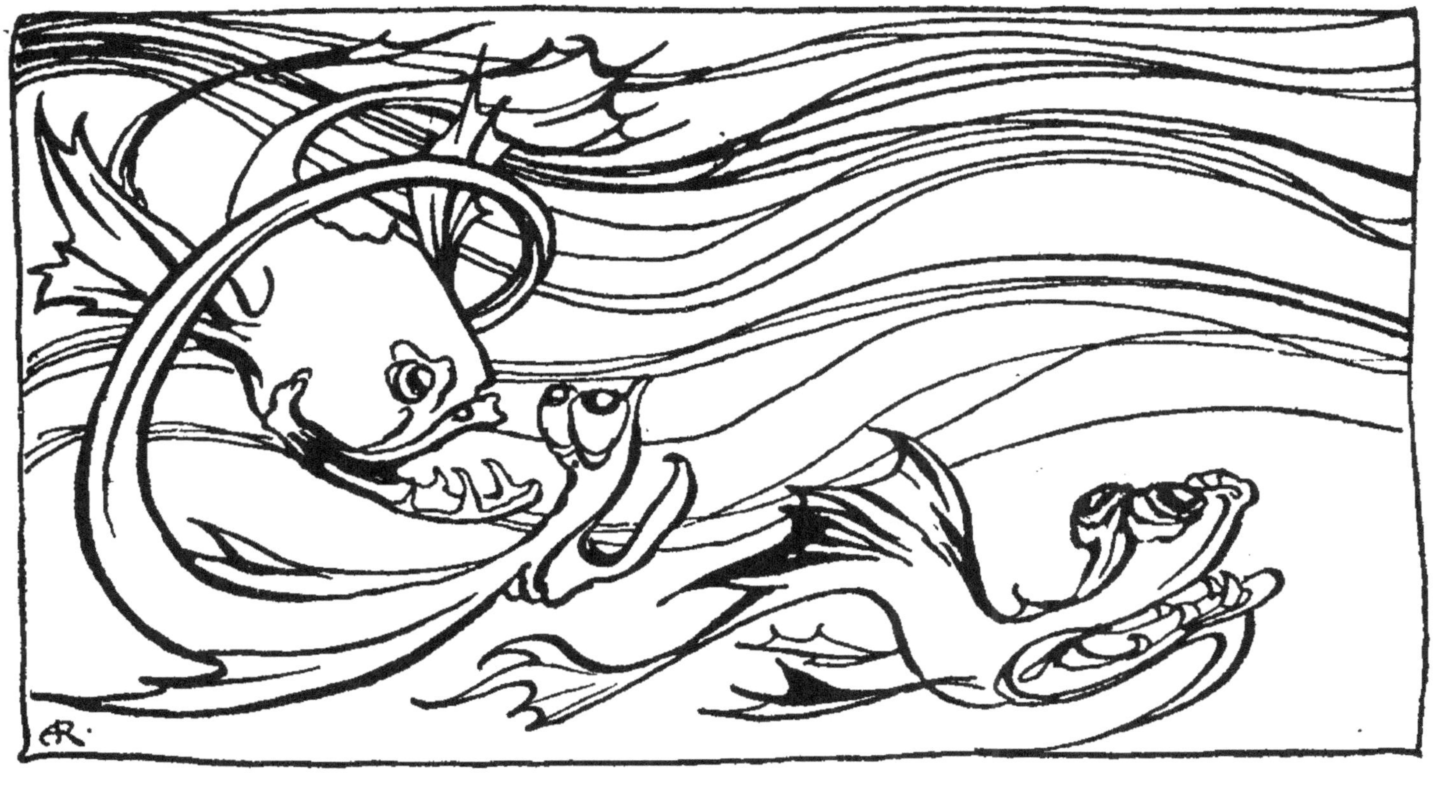

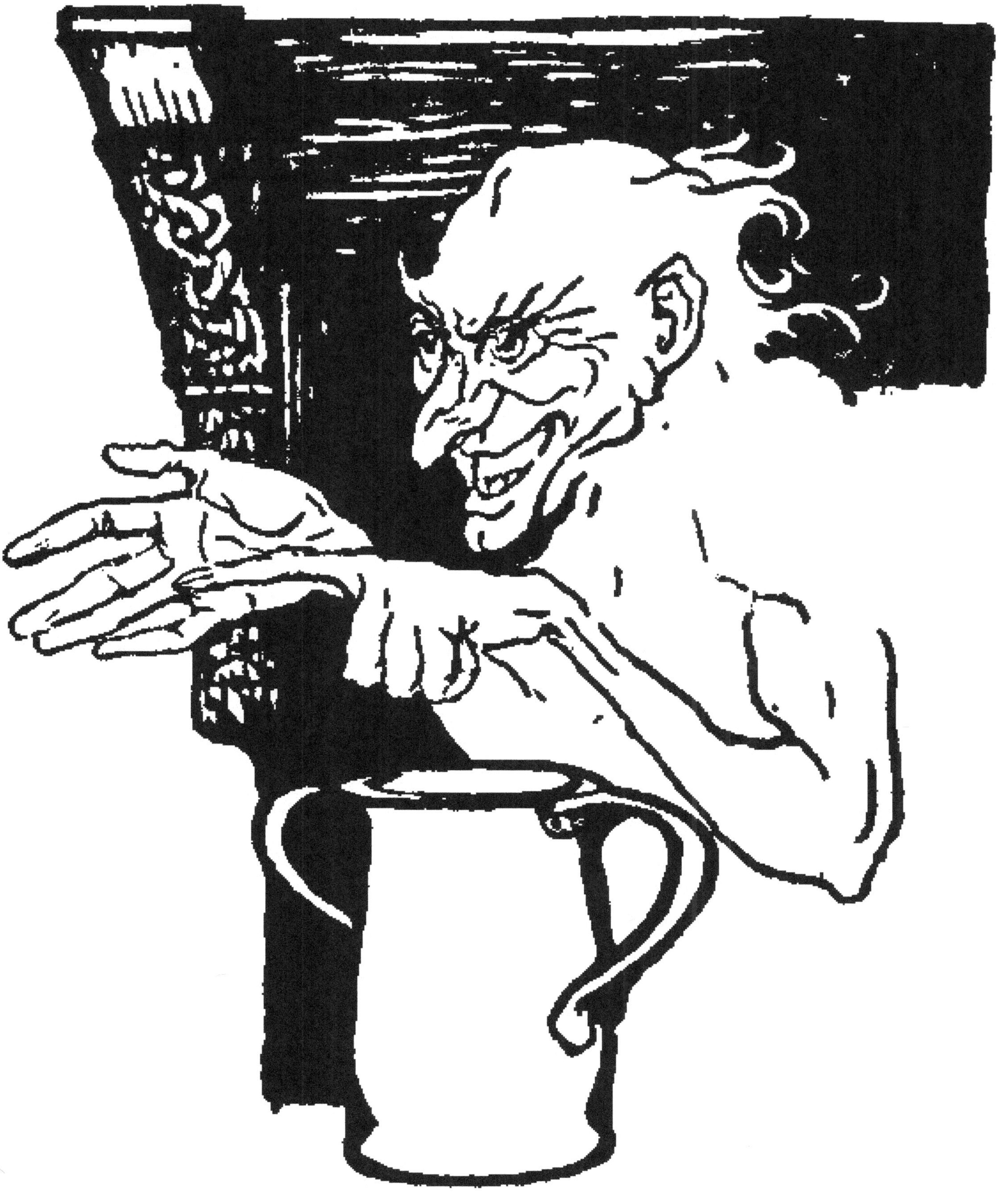

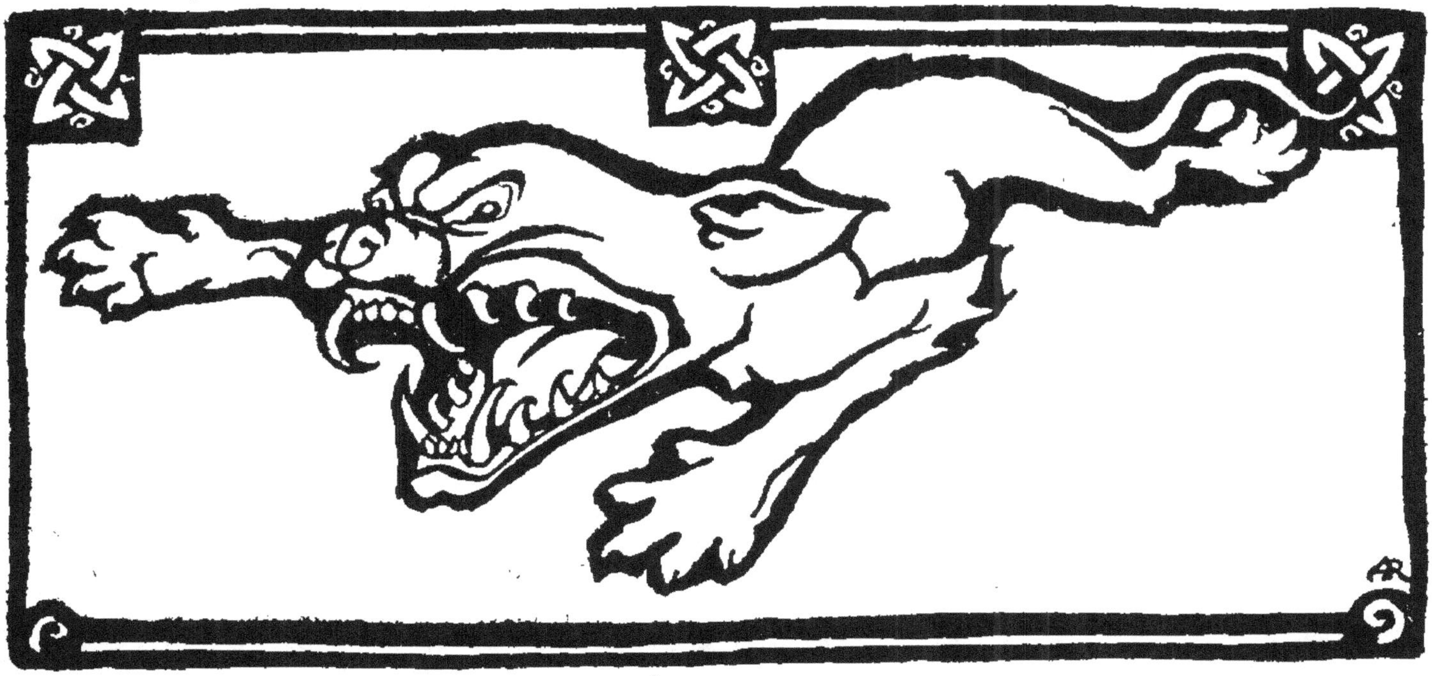

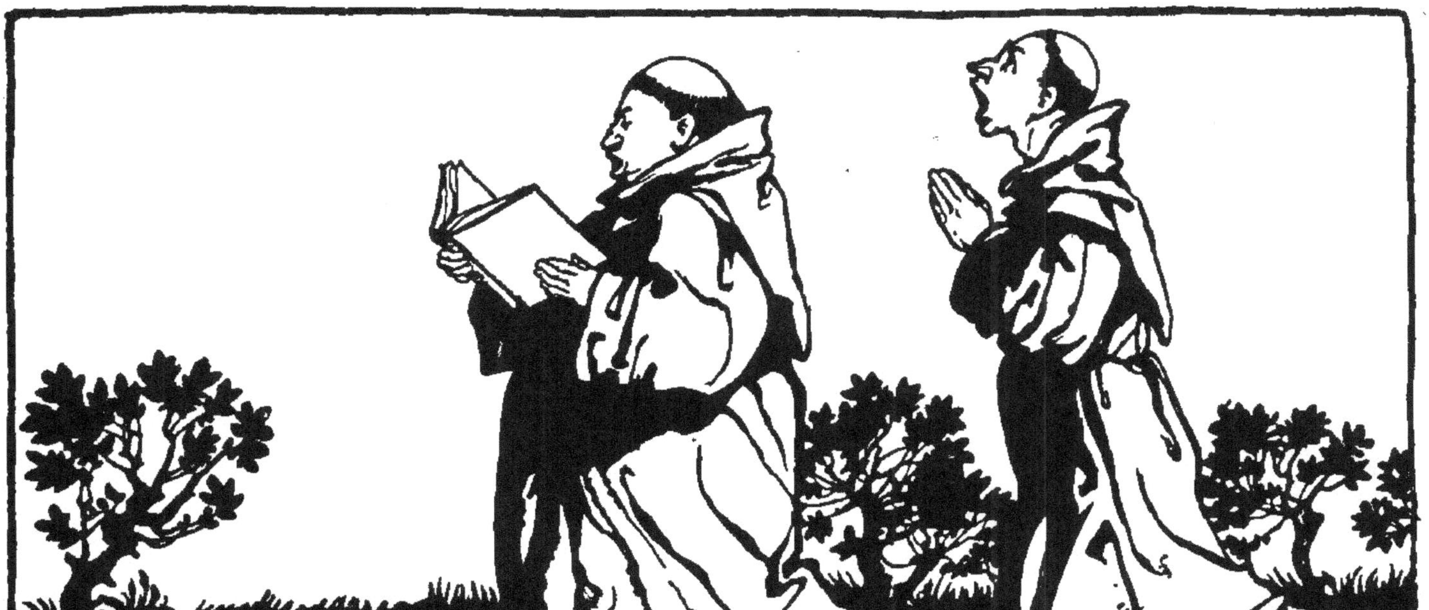

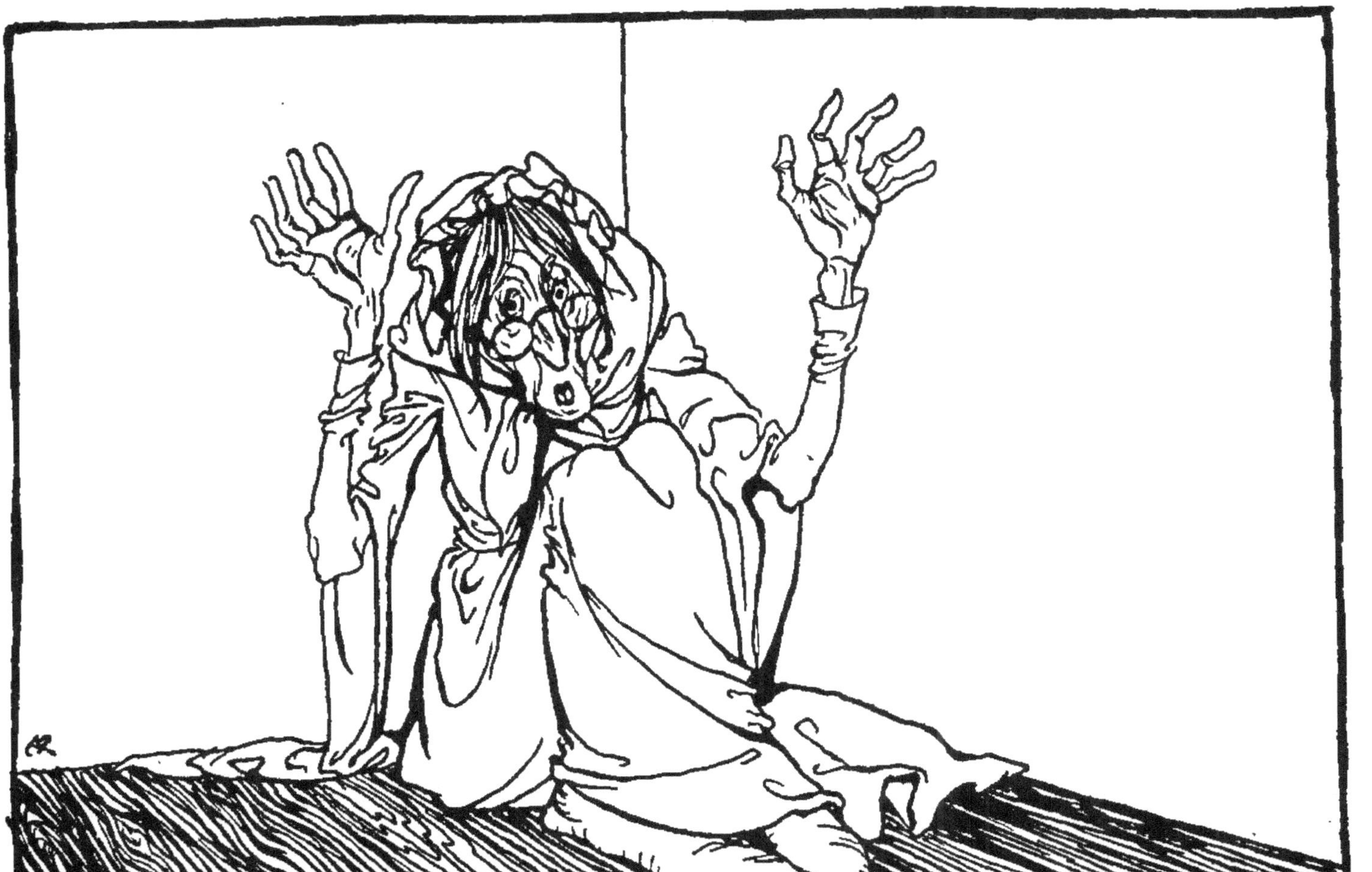

www.ingramcontent.com/pod-product-compliance
Lightning Source LLC
Chambersburg PA
CBHW082009230526
45468CB00023B/3003
* 9 7 8 1 7 2 0 9 9 5 8 1 4 *